SACRIFICE

HOWARD GUINNESS

InterVarsity Press
Downers Grove
Illinois 60515

Sixth edition

© 1975 by Inter-Varsity
Christian Fellowship of the
United States of America.

First published in Great Britain
by the Inter-Varsity Fellowship
of Evangelical Unions,
March 1936.

InterVarsity Press is the
book publishing division
of Inter-Varsity
Christian Fellowship.

The majority of Scripture
quotations are from the
Revised Standard Version
of the Bible, © 1946 and 1952
by the Division of Christian
Education of the National
Council of Churches.
Used by permission.

ISBN: 0-87784-307-4

Library of Congress Catalog
Card Number: 73-81575

Printed in the United
States of America

*This book is dedicated to the memory of my
mother, who lived this life of sacrifice, and to
the many university students in many lands whom
I am privileged to call my friends and who have
meant so much to me in my Christian life.*

CONTENTS

1/POVERTY _____ **9**

2/LOVE _____ **21**

3/DISCIPLINE _____ **43**

4/EXPERIENCE_____ **57**

5/POWER _____ **75**

EPILOGUE _____ **81**

Preface to the Sixth Edition

This booklet was first written when I was thirty-three years of age and had been involved for eight years in the spread of Inter-Varsity to many English-speaking countries across the world. I am now retired from traveling and preaching and live in a mountain village writing. In old age I feel as fulfilled and as useful as I did in earlier days, and more peaceful! The spotlight is now on others.

When I wrote the preface to the fifth edition in 1960, I was very ill, my expectation of life being only a few years. But God intervened and cured me so that I was able to finish my ministry at St. Michael's, Vaucluse, Sydney, and retire in 1971. So it is a very grateful and rather feeble person who writes this preface and whose prayers follow the new booklet as it is read by those to whom the Spirit sends it.

We have a favourite saying in our household, "You may not be very far up but you must be climbing!" I'm not half as far up as I thought I was when I wrote the first edition. But I'm still climbing.

Howard Guinness
Green Pastures, Wenworth Falls
The Blue Mountains, N. S. W.
Australia
January 4, 1975

POVERTY

"BLESSED ARE THE POOR IN SPIRIT, FOR THEIRS IS THE KINGDOM OF HEAVEN."[1] □ "WHOEVER OF YOU DOES NOT RENOUNCE ALL THAT HE HAS CANNOT BE MY DISCIPLE."[2]

On graduation, one of my friends at the hospital where I was training became a medical missionary. A number of years later, now a sick man, he set up practice in Australia. When I met him again in 1955 he was earning an excellent annual income and had built a large and attractive room onto his house for the purpose of holding meetings and services for the non-Christians of his outlying suburb. But when he succeeded in getting another Christian to come and take over this unique work he went off to overseas missionary work again!

The financial side never seemed to enter very much into his calculations. Nor the health side. He had one basic passion, which was to seek and find the lost.

This is what I mean by the spirit of poverty.

Or here is another man who illustrates the same thing. An M.Sc. of the University of Sydney accepted a position in industry with a well-known firm. (While at the university he had helped organize the evangelistic mission of 1951 when the Evangelical Union so captured the imagination of the university that leading rationalists attended aftermeetings and the Newman Society [Roman Catholic] publicly acknowledged its gratitude.) Soon he was earning a very good salary, with the promise of much more to follow. He liked his work, was liked by his colleagues and was a living witness for Christ each day among them.

But he resigned his position to enter a theological college and gave a farewell party to which he invited the rest of the management to explain to them his real ambition in life. He then spent three years grinding away at exams and eventually started to earn less than a third of his former salary. Three years later, his salary has risen no more than a fraction, although he also receives a house, wedding fees and a car allowance in addition to his salary. He is wholly immersed in the work and is supremely happy.

Another case is a woman science graduate who held an important position with the Commonwealth Scientific and Industrial Research Organization in Sydney. She was earning a salary appropriate to her highly skilled post and was known as a convinced Christian.

But she had a talent, her linguistic ability, which

she was not using and which she felt more and more must be used. Nor could she forget the many who had not once heard the gospel. So, after much thought and prayer, she resigned her position and entered the School of Linguistics in Melbourne. Today she is helping as a tutor in the school, training hard for the mission field and hoping eventually to be able to reduce to writing the languages of certain tribes living in New Guinea and thus to pave the way for them to read the Bible for themselves.

She does not look upon this as sacrifice but regards it simply as the path of duty and thus her greatest privilege.

Vocation

Such actions have the atmosphere of romance about them. Most of us, however, are asked to do the commonplace, and do it well. Let us throw ourselves, therefore, into our appointed task, doing it with all our might, and thereby bring glory to God. We must have very definite guidance before we resign a job in the belief that we are called to witness overseas. But would we be willing to go were such a call to come? That's the point. Moreover, would we be willing to go without prospect of returning home again? If the climate were such that it did not demand our retirement for health's sake at regular intervals, and if others were efficiently making known at home the needs of the foreign field from firsthand knowledge, would we be willing to go, and live, and die overseas?

Every Moravian and Roman Catholic missionary does this.

A student once wrote to me and suggested that one of the things which attracted him to a missionary's life was the furlough! Are we like that? I am not suggesting that God wants many of us to go, and stay, and never return. I think this is extremely improbable. But we must face the possibility of such a desire on his part and be willing to say, "Here am I, send me."

How much are we still governed by our natural likes and dislikes? How far have we been captivated by the spirit of the Crucified? It is often difficult to get young evangelical pastors to go and work in the slums or in poor churches. Once an evangelical minister in the north of England remarked to me that he could count on the fingers of one hand the clergymen in that part of the country who were doing soul-winning work. We are likely to be guided by a desire to work among a class of people to whom we are naturally attracted and in surroundings that are naturally congenial. If Christ had been guided that way, he would never have left heaven's glory for the sin and selfishness of this earth of ours: He would never have chosen the path of shame and suffering which led to Calvary.

Nationality and Class
A missionary leader in a foreign country was asked by the authorities whether he would be willing to be naturalized in order to live more perfectly with the nationals as *one of themselves* and show them Christ.

This country was not highly civilized in any sense, and in many respects it was primitive. Could he not sufficiently show them Christ without *that*? Could he not preach Christ and serve them with deeds of kindness and sacrifice to show them he loved them with the love of Christ? *Could* he—after such a request had been made by them? What was the love of Christ? What love did he want to show them? It was the love which made Christ willing to be naturalized and become a citizen of earth—one with a race of sinners and slaves. The Son of *man* was his favorite title for himself, not Son of *God* (although he was that). He took "the form of a servant, being born in the likeness of men."[3] After careful thought and prayer the missionary leader decided to be naturalized.

Are we willing to follow this far, if we are sure that Jesus is beckoning us on? Are we following him *now* in spirit along this path? When we meet the foreigner in our land, how do we think of him—as foreigner or brother? How do we look upon those of another class, those who have not been privileged with the upbringing or education we have had? How do we treat them? Are we one with them in the common bond of humanity or separated in spirit by the artificial barriers of a non-Christian world thinking non-Christian thoughts?

"He is not ashamed to call them brethren"![4]

Possessions

A bachelor clergyman used to invite the "down and

outs" to share his quarters with him, eat his food and accept his friendship if they would. The utter inadequacy of offering them a few dollars had burnt its way into his soul and he went a step further, which brought him very near not only to those he wanted to help but to Christ himself. "Inasmuch . . ."[5] became suddenly real. Of course, he met frauds who stole his belongings, but he met far more who went away praising God that at last they had seen and felt the love of Christ; and he himself learned to take joyfully the spoiling of his goods.[6]

A Cambridge man, who later went overseas to do pioneer missionary work, used to bicycle each year to the Keswick Convention (an annual conference promoting the deeper Christian life held each summer at Keswick in England's Lake District), sustaining himself on the way with the simplest of food. He had money to travel by either car or train and eat in first-class hotels, but he felt that it would be unchristian for him to do this. He chose to follow his Master closely in practical ways as he prepared for a life of service and hardship. Today he is a man full of the Holy Spirit and power, having learned to obey *in little things*. It is *willingness* for simplicity that God wants us to have, though he may often allow us greater luxury than our bare needs demand.

It is important to add here, however, that it is the principle which matters. God may guide certain Christians to dine in hotels and restaurants for special purposes, not least of which may be that someone else is there, prepared for the gospel and waiting for the messenger.

If we are one of the happy ones who are renounced in spirit,[7] the problem of possessions will solve itself. There will be no desire to be anything other than simple and unostentatious in clothes, hobbies, habits and food. Our ambition will be to serve, not to be served; to give, not to get. There will be no desire to go one better than our next-door neighbor in any direction that the world, the flesh or the devil might suggest. We shall automatically avoid habits and hobbies which cost a lot either to start or maintain, quite apart from the question of whether or not we are able to afford them. Only overwhelming guidance from God will persuade us to touch them, and then we shall take care that the amount we spend on them is under his control too. We shall live as simply and cheaply as is compatible with the station in life God has given us and be prepared to break with any conventions which hinder us from doing so.

Regular Self-Denial

A lady I know, whose large family had scattered all over the earth and whose husband was dead, went to live close to one of her sons in an English village. She spent a very small amount per week on her food while working among the villagers and taking Christ to them; at the same time she is known to have given well over three thousand times her weekly food bill to a missionary society. This was only discovered accidentally after her death. She stinted herself and lived in the utmost simplicity so she could give liberally where she knew there was need. But she never stinted others, far less her children, even though this attitude toward money was her life's attitude.

Are we giving only out of surplus? Why shouldn't we start to follow her example in some small degree? The woman long ago who gave *at great sacrifice* to the temple fund gave more than all the wealthier patrons whose giving actually cost them little.[8] A practice of regular self-denial and fasting, if carried out in the spirit of humility, will do at least three good things: (1) strengthen our characters, (2) strengthen our bodies and (3) save money for God's work.

Vacations

Most of us could save on vacation trips and yet have just as restful and enjoyable a time. Surely from every point of view they should be as inexpensive as is compatible with the rest we require? On one occasion I was given the privilege of a holiday in Switzerland with my brother, through the kindness of some friends. That holiday was a great physical boon. I feel strongly, however, that were such an offer made to me again I would decline it (unless a real invalid) and seek the needed rest closer to home, and at less than a quarter of the cost. It seems to me to be one of those things which (for me) must be classed as "lawful but not helpful."[9] For there is the possibility that this "liberty" might become a stumbling-block to those who are weak.[10] Further, there is an urgent need for a gesture to be made by a section of God's church to draw people's attention to the avoidable wastage which is going on. Money spent on luxuries, little or big, which, in the face of the crying need of the world and the extreme difficulty experienced by missionary societies in finding funds, is criminal!

"Sell All That Thou Hast"

A Cambridge man who was a member of the university flying club owned a beautiful airplane of his own, of which he was justly proud. But he discovered that the plane had become his idol and, although equipped with unusual gifts as a pilot, he sold it and restored Christ to the place of preeminence in his life. An Oxford man sold his sports car so that he could give the money to God's work at a moment when it was badly needed. Another sold his camera and an unnecessary blazer to give the money to the mission field; and others in various walks of life have sold larger or smaller things which they know they can do without in order to come as close as possible in their own appointed station in life to the One who had nowhere to lay his head. A mighty army of his followers down through the ages has resolutely refused to possess anything which might be termed by the world an unnecessary luxury and therefore compromising to their Christian profession. We must recapture that spirit today. Life for some has become too easy and, even for those who do not have many luxuries, too far removed from the simplicity of our Savior.

If we are to carry this out, it will probably mean selling at a loss. It's worth it. Indeed, with some of our possessions which are unsaleable, it is worthwhile to give them away if we can give them to those who will really profit by them. The gain to us in spiritual power, and to them in material possession, makes it a good investment every time.

On the other hand, some are called to work among the educated or wealthy and therefore must live in such a way as to be able to influence them. It is the *spirit* of poverty that is essential. Also, there are those who have comforts and luxuries not so much for their own sakes as for those whom they invite to share them. They are holding their worldly goods in real stewardship. There are others, however, who should probably spend more on themselves and give away less! They are slovenly or careless in their dress and thus bring dishonor on the Name they love; while some have even become selfish in their unselfishness and self-indulgent in their sacrifice. Let's use common sense in these matters, and be strict with ourselves, not with others.

Tithing

Gairdner of Cairo exemplified throughout his life another duty to God. He tithed his income. Speaking of the early days of the Student Movement, he says, "We were in such deadly earnest that we not only did not spare ourselves, we did not spare one another, if

we thought we saw signs of obstinacy or exaggeration
or snobbishness. We were all living hard and giving
every penny we could save to missions. I remember
A. G. Fraser being taken to task for having gold waist-
coat buttons!"[11] And one of his friends says about an
address of his on "Giving," "That address changed
the character of the Movement. I don't suppose any of
the men who heard it ever again gave so little as a
tenth. It sent me back to Oxford not only to pay my
debts, but to live on half of what I had lived on before."

The question we must ask ourselves here is, Do we
give even a tenth of our money to the Lord's work?
A Cambridge man said to me lately that he found he
was unable to afford contributing a tenth of his allowance in this way and still remain "up." The solution
he had found was to give a twentieth directly and a
twentieth indirectly by working at camps and missions.

If we are among those, however, who are not yet
earning money for ourselves and are living on an
allowance, we must make sure that our parents agree
with our using their money in this way, or, if we are
receiving a government grant, that we are using the
money wisely and for the purposes for which it has
been given to us. The most scrupulous honesty is
necessary here. God knows our circumstances and
how much, or how little, we can give. But he also
knows that almost all of us could give more if we were
to form proper habits of giving.

It is important, too, that our giving be regular. It is a good plan to have a special fund into which we place a certain proportion of all the money we receive. This is money to be spent directly on God's work and is "sacred." Having done this, however, let's not consider our other money as "secular" or as our own. All is his; we are but stewards.[12]

Accounts

Most will find a conscientious keeping of private accounts, balanced every day or two, to be a help toward a life of simplicity and economy. It is good, too, to check our weekly or monthly expenditure with someone else who is trying to live the same sort of life and will not be easy on us. It will need someone who, understanding our circumstances, will really take the trouble to look into our accounts and hold us to the highest.

"Blessed are the poor in spirit, for theirs is the kingdom of heaven."[13]

LOVE

"GREATER LOVE HAS NO MAN THAN THIS, THAT A MAN LAY DOWN HIS LIFE FOR HIS FRIENDS."[1] □ "DO YOU LOVE ME MORE THAN THESE?"[2]

This chapter, like the rest of the book, is written to lovers of the Lord Jesus. They know something of his love which passes knowledge and have started to judge all loves by that sublime standard. To them love is no longer simply a thing of the flesh, but of the spirit. Spiritual kinship has begun to mean more to them than mental and physical. A pretty face or a fascinating mind now comes second to a Christ-like spirit. They judge *spiritually*.

Christian Love

When the love of Christ comes into a human life, it is the greatest uplifting and ennobling power of which the world has any knowledge. It brings *new birth*, for it brings Christ himself.[3] For this love no sacrifice is too great, no piece of service too humble. It seeks out the lonely and friendless and gives itself unsparingly whether there is any appreciation of the sacrifice or not. It seeks the lost sheep, to bring them back to the Shepherd. It lays down its life for the sheep. It is God's love, revealed in Christ, and shed abroad in our hearts by the Holy Spirit.

Hear the apostle Paul describing its virtues: "This love of which I speak is slow to lose patience—it looks for a way of being constructive. It is not possessive; it is neither anxious to impress nor does it cherish inflated ideas of its own importance.

"Love has good manners and does not pursue selfish advantage. It is not touchy. It does not keep account of evil or gloat over the wickedness of other people. On the contrary, it is glad with all good men when truth prevails.

"Love knows no limit to its endurance, no end to its trust, no fading of its hope; it can outlast anything. It is, in fact, the one thing that still stands when all else has fallen."[4]

Have you ever received this gift of God's love? Have you received Jesus Christ as Savior? If not, you are still dead in your sins[5] and know nothing of divine love.[6]

Human Love
Few greater blessings can come to a Christian man or woman than the love of another whom God has

chosen to be their life partner. Few greater responsibilities can come, either. A real Christian home is the nearest approach we have to heaven this side of the grave. Blessed of God indeed are those to whom he entrusts this great treasure!

"When two souls really discover each other, then at once a new life begins, so radiant, beautiful, stimulating, and mysterious, that even the poets have failed to find sufficient words for it. In their hearts two lovers always know that this is what they were made for —that this is the very core and essence of human existence."[7]

But the power of sex, which can lift us to the highest heights, can also bring us to the deepest depths. "Contrast," says a modern writer, "these two sets of words and the ideas behind them—parental care, chivalry, sacrifice, and art, with lust, jealousy, and prostitution. By sex we become capable of the highest and finest of human achievements, and by sex we can sink to a lower level of life than that of the unreasoning animal world. It is a mighty power within us for good or ill, for weal or woe."[8] It is because of this that we must consider in this chapter some of the problems of love and friendship which many of us may be facing at this present moment.

In the pages which follow, while recognizing the vital difference between friendship and the love which is to find its goal in marriage, I do not always differentiate clearly between them in their early stages. No one can infallibly. What starts as a perfectly

ordinary friendship often goes on to become a very
real love. I have known a sharp Christian fellow who
was uncertain about whether it was real love until the
day he asked the girl to marry him! On the other hand,
some who fall in love quickly and feel certain that
theirs is the real thing awaken later to discover that it
is not, that they have been bowled over by a pretty
face or a charming personality. It has been largely not
a *spiritual love*, but a natural fascination. Of course,
the natural and physical must come into it, but where
they predominate and fail to develop into anything
more spiritual, trouble arises.

How, then, can I be certain that I am really in love?
The first important thing to say, I think, is that a satis-
factory answer on paper is extraordinarily difficult. So
for some of you what I say now will not help very
much. For others it may help a little.

Bryan Green has six test questions which clear the
ground somewhat, and I would like to add a seventh.
Here they are:

1. How long have you known each other? Long
enough to study each other and understand something of each other's mind, habits and spirit?

2. In what circumstances have you known each
other? Only in the more dramatic, spectacular and
appealing (holidays, evenings out, social and religious functions, etc.) or in the prosaic relationships
of the home as well?

3. What do you miss most when separated? the
physical or the mental and spiritual? If it is the physi-

cal, then think again.

4. What common interests and background have you? The "thrill" of love may bring you together but it won't hold you together. The comradeship of love will have to outlast many days in which there are no thrills.

5. Do you share common ideals and faith? The sort of love that can make a success of marriage must have these in common not only for your own happiness but also for your children's. It will affect the day-to-day way you bring them up. To be pulling in two different directions where they are concerned, whether in things little or big, will be disastrous.

6. Do you trust each other absolutely? Life will bring its storms and you must have complete confidence in each other if you are to weather them successfully.

7. Do you admire the other's character? If you do not deeply respect and admire each other, forget about marriage. You are not in love.

Quite obviously "it is not enough that merely to look at 'her' makes your blood run fast and your nerves tingle. It is not enough that the very sight of 'him' should give you acute pleasure. Before a man and woman get engaged, they would do well to have some long talks together, and so to find out what their real interests are, and whether their general views and purposes in life are such as can possibly be harmonized. Marriage lasts for a long time, and it is a poor affair when a husband is bored by his wife's conversation, or when a wife is repelled by her husband's views!"[9]

"Love is blind, but marriage is an eye opener!" quotes a friend of mine who has a sense of humor and a charming wife. "You never really know anyone until you have lived with them intimately for several months at least, and, finally, nothing but love will get you through the 'tiffs' which may come."

But love cannot be analyzed! We each must tread this joyous, difficult and dangerous path alone and find out for ourselves. Happy is the man or woman, therefore, who knows the Guide and trusts that Guide, for in him and his sure guidance lies the only solution to this problem. God can lead me to the person of his choice. Wise then is he who spends time each day with Christ and ensures that for that day at least he is near enough to him to be kept on the narrow path.

Another problem of love is in its very strength. Sometimes we may be so taken up with another person that we become thoughtlessly selfish or less efficient at our work, because our whole being is monopolized by the wonder of our amazing discovery. A man who hoped to serve God abroad used to meet his fiancée regularly for the purpose of learning the language. Their progress, however, was not as fast as they had hoped, because their brains worked at different speeds and the faster of the two never needed to exert himself. It is possible that they would have worked better separately. Their primary motive in working together was love, although they may have felt at the time it was progress. Older friends felt that there would have been better work and a truer love had their times of meeting been more disciplined.

The fact is that lack of discipline in our love is sometimes hidden under the cloak of religion. We meet together for prayer and Bible study, and sometimes the amount of real work that gets done is small and the main memory carried away is of the other. We sit together in church and enjoy each other's company, sometimes to the exclusion of true worship and often to the exclusion of bringing someone else to hear the gospel. Let us then sift our motives and see that our love does not become selfish.

Human Friendships

"The mutual relations of men and women in the realm of comradeship, and quite apart from marriage, may be so happy and enriching—so exhilarating and so bracing—that one may reverently say the whole arrangement of having divided mankind into two such groups is one of the most splendid of the divine thoughts. . . . In all life's departments, with a few obvious exceptions, men and women supplement and stimulate one another, and by comradeship make a bigger and better thing of life than would be possible otherwise."[10]

Isolated Friendships If we want to achieve fine friendships, however, we have no easy task before us, for the pitfalls are many. Just as it is possible to spoil the beauty of love with selfishness and lack of discipline, so it is in our friendships. Moreover, in an isolated friendship we always run the risk of one person falling in love while the other still continues to think of the relation merely as a friendship. As long, however, as neither has been guilty of leading the other on to expect something more than comradeship, the suffering that comes, although acute, may be redemptive if used in the right way. There are many who believe that, despite the risk, friendships between the sexes are too valuable to be abandoned. It has, however, been pointed out that the risk is made unnecessarily great if we have one friend of the opposite sex and only one. It would appear that until we feel guided by God to seek a friendship which may lead to marriage, it is better to have several friends of the opposite sex or none at all.

Selfish Friendships A medical friend of mine, finding that he was spending too much time with a girl friend during his medical studies, talked things over with her and together they came to the conclusion that they ought to concentrate on their appointed jobs and spend less time together. This they did at real sacrifice, but with an increase of joy and fruitfulness that made it very worthwhile.

Much time, money and enthusiasm is sometimes spent on a legitimate friendship which we think may one day lead to engagement and marriage. Such a friendship may either help or hinder the spiritual life of those concerned. If it is sacrificial, it will help; if possessive, it will hinder. The trouble with many of our friendships is that they are self-centered. When I say I am fond of someone else, how much is it real affection for that person and how much a possessive sentiment which is more concerned with my own enjoyment than with the welfare of the other? With some of us it is largely because someone gives us their affection that we give ours in return. The other person gives us a thrill; we love the sensation and we love possessing such a friendship for what we get out of it. Is not the logical conclusion, therefore, that *we love ourselves*? This is not true of all friendships, of course, and not totally true of any, but it applies enough to be stated here so that we will guard our friendships carefully from becoming self-centered.

A self-centered friendship breeds jealousy and discontent. Such a friendship is therefore a real hindrance to the happiness and usefulness of an individual, while a disciplined friendship is as great a help as the other is a hindrance. I know the experience of losing my first love for Christ because affection for another took its place. The Bible and prayer both became unreal because the image of the friend was always in front of me and between me and God. Time, money and enthusiasm were spent on what was to prove a tenth-rate and over-emotional friendship. Even a second-rate one is not worthy, for "nothing but the best" must be the standard of the disciple who is called to follow such a Master as Christ. Some friendships have to be altered in their emphasis,

others radically changed. This one had to go alto-
gether.

Engagement

An engagement should not be short, except in the case
of those who have known each other for several years
already. For others it is a period of testing and adjust-
ment and confirmation of the choice made. If instead
of confirmation there should arise a persistent doubt
in the mind of either as to the rightness of going forward to marriage, then a visit to their minister or to
a marriage counsellor or to some wise and instructed
Christian friend should clear up the matter. But such
a visit should be arranged prayerfully in full depen-
dence on the Lord to give the guidance needed.

Far better a broken engagement—broken at the last
moment, if necessary—than a marriage outside the
will of God.

Broken Engagements

Why do we find broken engagements so often in
Christian circles? Don't they bring discredit on the
Name we love? Don't they in many cases mean broken
hearts? The cause can usually be traced to one or more
of the following: (1) The undue haste of a life not fully
under the control of God's Holy Spirit. (2) An overwhelming physical attraction (lacking the qualities of
true love) with its consequent desire of gaining im-
mediate happiness for oneself. (3) Lack of sex instruc-
tion by the parents, with a consequent mental and

physical revolt when the facts become known.[11] "I would rather have all the risks which come from a free discussion of sex than the greater risks we run by a conspiracy of silence," a former Archbishop of Canterbury once said.

Unsanctified Engagements

A man called to go to the mission field becomes engaged to a girl who has not received that call and does not receive that call. They marry and do Christian work at home. It is possible, I know, that the man's original "call" may have been mistaken enthusiasm and his ultimate work the right one. But it may not have been so; he may have put his desire for earthly joy before his desire for a share in his Master's sufferings, poverty and loneliness. He may have chosen both for himself and another—second-best. In this connection it is interesting to read in Mrs. Howard Taylor's book, *The Triumph of John and Betty Stam*,[12] how utterly surrendered to Christ this side of their life was: "She was leaving Chicago and had applied for membership in the China Inland Mission. If accepted, she would go out in a few months. John had another year at Moody's. He was not yet sure about China. . . . He could not ask Betty to commit herself to an engagement when his way might not open to follow her to China. And more than this, even if his going proved to be of the Lord, what about the life of hardship as a pioneer evangelist? He might be in the work which would preclude his marrying for some years. Would it be fair to ask Betty to wait indefinitely?"

To Betty the path was plain: "God had called her to China and had opened the way. John's future was still uncertain. If health or other circumstances kept him at home, she could not turn back from her life work. They had seen something of the sorrow and loss that had come to others through not seeking 'first the kingdom of God,' through letting down spiritual standards and losing 'the heavenly vision.' "

To his father, John wrote, "Betty knows that, in all fairness and love to her, I cannot ask her to enter into an engagement with years to wait. But we can have a real understanding, keeping the interests of the Lord's work always first.

"The China Inland Mission has appealed for men, single men, to itinerate in sections where it would be impossible to take a woman, until more settled work has been commenced. . . . Some time ago I promised the Lord that, if fitted for this forward movement, I would gladly go into it, so now I cannot back down without sufficient reason, merely upon personal considerations. If, after we are out a year or two, we find the Lord's work would be advanced by our marriage, we need not wait longer.

"From the way I have written, you and others might think that I was talking about a cartload of lumber, instead of something that has dug down very deep into our hearts. Betty and I have prayed much about this, and I am sure that, if our sacrifice is unnecessary, the Lord will not let us miss any of His blessings. Our hearts are set to do His will. . . . But this is true, isn't it, our wishes must not come first? The progress of the Lord's work is the chief consideration. So there are times when we just have to stop and think hard."

Too narrow a path for us to tread? "Narrow is the way that leads to *life*, and few there be that find it."[13] It depends whether you want *life* or are satisfied with existence—the existence of a second-best. The words of Mr. Stam, as he read John's letter, apply to all who are taking this narrow path: "Those children are going to have God's choicest blessing."

It is not even uncommon to find men who have become foreign missionaries entering upon hasty and unsuitable engagements and marriages. They realize that the number of women in their mission is limited, and the number who attract them is more limited still. Therefore, they try to snap up the most likely one in case delay might prove "fatal." Let the impetuous man move slowly here. Far better months of agonized waiting and uncertainty than years of regret or a settling down into a groove of the commonplace to make the best of it, enjoying any happiness that may come his way.

There are some men, however, who have kept the woman they love waiting far too long. They have become cowardly in their indecision, and cruel too. One day they will wake up to the just recompense of their procrastination—the inability to decide or even the death of the love which once drew them on so irresistibly.

We started this chapter on a high plane. It would have been possible to speak first about those who have become engaged to worldly Christians or to people who are not truly Christians at all. Being attracted they deliberately allowed themselves to fall in love and eventually to marry, thus becoming lost to the cause of Christ. Most of us know of such cases. They are common tragedies in the Christian church and one of the serious points of leakage in vital Christian circles today. And they will continue until we can live close enough to the Lord Jesus to leave the future in his hands and not search around for a life partner, knowing that he will bring us together in his own time and in his own way, if we will only let him. Oh, that we might take the advice of the singer who three times breaks in upon the songs of the bride and bridegroom in the Song of Songs with the same words:

I adjure you, O daughters of Jerusalem,
   by the gazelles or the hinds of the field,
that you stir not up nor awaken love
   until it please.[14]

G. Campbell Morgan adds in his *Living Messages*, "I would that this interrupting charge might be inscribed in letters of fire, and hung in every hall where young people assemble."[15] The fact that many husbands and wives are not happy and that many just barely manage to get along with each other and make a show of it before the world should be a warning against deliberately trying to awaken love. This warning is emphasized by the far too numerous "separated" families, where the strain of living together has become too great. It is reinforced by the divorces which are the logical outcome of marrying in a hurry, largely because of a physical attraction, and finding out at leisure that this is an insufficient basis for marriage where the mental and spiritual outlooks are so different that they are mutually unsatisfying.

The Problem
There is, then, a threefold problem:

1. Selfish friendships which absorb time, money and enthusiasm that, during the days of training, would be better spent in getting more fully prepared for our life work or given directly to the Lord.

2. Broken engagements which dishonor the Lord and often leave behind bitterness and broken hearts.

3. Unsanctified engagements and marriages which lead either party into second-best for his or her life and rob God of his own possessions, which keep many prospective missionaries at home every year and which may bring in their train unhappiness or even separation and divorce.

The Remedy
Because of the seriousness of the problem, I suggest a costly remedy which I believe will help eradicate this cancer which is causing so much spiritual coldness and death. It is contained in the following principles:

1. A person should not seriously consider the formation of a friendship with a person of the other sex with a view to marriage until he has settled down to his life work.

2. Having accepted this principle, he should hold by it unless he receives overwhelming guidance from God to the contrary—guidance which is confirmed by the advice of others who are living the same sort of life.

3. A man or woman should be willing never to marry if it becomes plain that this is God's will for them.

4. A man or woman should marry only a person who will be a real partner in the work of the Lord. Their married life should, by God's grace, be disciplined and unselfish, and their home open to all who need their friendship and love.

Objections

A number of objections to these suggestions immediately present themselves.

1. *How can I be sure that, if I wait, some other man will not win the girl I love?*

I want to suggest that it is reasonable to trust God to keep for me the girl he has planned to become my life partner. If I were to lose the one whom at present I want to marry, would it not be proof that God had not chosen that girl for me, and could I not praise him for saving me from accepting second-best? If, after waiting, he were to bring us together, would it not be an added proof that this was indeed his choice; and would we not go forward into the future with even greater assurance and joy? This actually happened to one of my friends. The girl refused the proposals of several men while he waited. God was keeping her for him, and they are now married happily.

2. *That is all very well for the man, but what about the girl? The man has the initiative in his hands while the girl has to wait to be spoken to before ever being certain if love is returned. Might not such a course involve a great deal of suffering and wondering for her?*

Yes, it might indeed, unless a definite understanding were arrived at between them. It is good for a man to remember that a woman is not only different from him physically but also emotionally and mentally. What has little effect upon him may affect her strangely, and vice versa. If it is possible for a real and mutually satisfying understanding to be arrived at—good. If not, then the course of action I have suggested cannot be adopted. But if they both seek God's guidance, he will surely lead them into his own perfect will for their lives, if they are willing to follow. If, however, the man becomes aware of her attraction for him and decides not to encourage it, there is obviously nothing more to be said.

3. *Might not such an attitude toward the other sex mean growing up utterly ignorant of it and therefore quite incapable of choosing a life partner intelligently? Might it not mean that the first attractive person who comes on the scene after the barrier has been let down, whether*

suitable or not, will capture the heart of one ignorant of
the other sex and thus produce the exact situation from
which the barrier was expected to deliver?

Yes, of course. Such a result might certainly come
about. There will be no need for this to happen, however, if the danger is recognized and guarded against
by the cultivation and enjoyment of friendships with
the other sex in the natural course of everyday life.
This natural comradeship is of great importance and
is as valuable as those with our own sex. Segregation
is both unnatural and harmful; each sex has something to give and receive from the other.

Let us then use quite naturally any contacts with
the opposite sex which come our way in the ordinary
course of the day's work. Let us keep them, however,
on a high intellectual and spiritual plane (avoiding
silliness or mere frivolity, for each is worth more and
can give more than that) and let us observe the usual
healthy barriers which God has appointed between
the sexes. Let us become neither too distant nor too
familiar in our friendships. God will help us achieve
this happy balance if we ask him.

Such an attitude, of course, demands the deliberate
and planned avoidance of everything which tends to
set fire to the emotions. It demands a determination
of the *will* to avoid all sexual excitement. Don't fall
into the error of thinking that this is repression and
will produce harmful consequences. There is a world
of difference between suppression (self-control) and
repression. McDougall states clearly in his book, *Ener-*

gies of Man, the need for self-discipline (suppression) in a life of "integrity."[16] Repression is defined for us in popular language by a modern author as "the non-voluntary but purposed thrusting down into the unconscious mind of something which so long as it is conscious, is distasteful to the personality."[17] It is therefore an unconscious act. "To put it another way," he says, "the opposite of repression is not expression, it is conscious recognition. The opposite of suppression is expression." When this is thought through it becomes self-evident.

4. *Surely being engaged might be a very great help to certain types of people during the period mentioned?*

Yes, this is perfectly true. But we are asking such people for Christ's sake to abstain from entering an engagement because through it the "weaker brethren" might be caused to stumble. Are we willing to look upon even this as lawful but not expedient? Are we willing to go as far as Paul in his self-sacrifice when he said (and he undoubtedly acted on it when necessary), "If food is a cause of my brother's falling, I will never eat meat, lest I cause my brother to fall"; or again, "And so by your knowledge this weak man is destroyed, the brother for whom Christ died."[18] Can't we trust our heavenly Father to see that, because our motive is the highest, we shall not lose any of the good which might come to us through an earlier engagement?

5. *Isn't marriage the climax of all manhood and womanhood? Isn't this the legitimate goal to which I can look*

forward and for which I should aim?

In attempting to answer this question let's realize first that for some this ideal is unattainable. "There is a surplus of girls in the world and therefore there are some for whom that ideal development of the sex instinct is impossible. Then, unfortunately, too many men are busy with their careers and will not marry."[19] In addition, the economic conditions of the present day "bring forward difficulties in the building of a new home (for the sheltering of the new life that shall come)" which make many hesitate.

But, beyond this, we must face the fact that it may not be the will of God for us to marry. We can't say it is our inherent right, although it is obviously the ideal for most. We would do well to think much before speaking of "inherent rights" in any direction, remembering that we are not our own. Paul gloried in calling himself the "bond-slave"[20] of Jesus Christ; and the Roman slave had no rights of his own, he belonged to his master utterly. He also suggests that we should be content, as far as earthly things are concerned, with "food and clothing."[21] Of himself he said, "I have learned, in whatever state I am, to be content."[22] Christ promised to provide sufficient food and clothing for our needs only if we put first his kingdom and righteousness,[23] nothing more. How much happier to take everything from his hand as the gift of his love, unmerited and undeserved by us, rather than as our "right"!

The surrender to him of our unwillingness to follow

him often breaks down the last barrier to the indwelling Spirit, who then is free to flood our lives with his love and power. Several students I knew intimately never discovered the fullness of the power of the Holy Spirit until their unwillingness to go through life unmarried was surrendered to Christ. One of them, I remember especially, soon afterwards traveled alone a thousand miles to preach the gospel (it was a very unusual undertaking and he was no speaker) and was used by God to convert many unlikely people. To make such a surrender is not synonymous with a vow to be celibate, for to those who have done so God has often given a life-partner and the joys of parenthood *at his own time and in his own way.* It implies only the utter willingness to be such.[24]

"I appeal to you therefore, brethren, by the mercies of God, to present your bodies as a living sacrifice, holy and acceptable to God, which is your spiritual worship ... that you may prove what is the will of God, what is good and acceptable and perfect."[25]

DISCIPLINE

"THERE WILL BE NO REVIVAL OF RELIGION,"
SAYS NICOLAS BERDYAEV, THE GREAT RUSSIAN
CHRISTIAN PHILOSOPHER AND SEER, "UNTIL
THERE IS A REVIVAL OF THE ASCETIC LIFE IN
THE CHURCH OF JESUS CHRIST." □ "KEEP HOLD
OF DISCIPLINE, DO NOT LET GO; GUARD HER,
FOR SHE IS YOUR LIFE."[1]
The Oxford Dictionary says of discipline, "Training;
especially of the kind that produces self-control, or-
derliness, *obedience* and capacity for co-operation."

What would an army be like without discipline?
It could not work smoothly internally or be effective
against the enemy, and it would be a danger to those
for whose protection it existed. This is true of the undisciplined Christian. He is perpetually at war within himself, with the result that his offensive against
the enemy is ineffective and his influence on others
demoralizing. In the Christian ranks he is more trou-

ble than he is worth.

The effective Christian is disciplined in every part of his personality and being—mind, heart, will, body and spirit.

The Spirit and God

Secret Prayer J. H. Oldham in his *Devotional Diary*, which provided space for recording each day the time spent in quiet prayer, says that such a record is "an aid against self-deception ... and enables one to know how far one's actual practice accords with one's accepted standards in a matter of vital importance."[2] Are we deceiving ourselves here? How long do we *actually* spend in prayer? Some of us might be disgusted with ourselves if we put down on paper the amount of time we gave to prayer each day last week. Must it be said of us as it was of certain others long ago, "Practise and observe whatever they tell you, but not what they do; for they preach, but do not practise"?[3]

Humility and Love Lack of humility before God (not merely the acceptance of the fact that I am nothing but the practical realization of the fact) and lack of love for both God and man spring from pride, and lead on to criticism. This spirit continues to split our ranks and discredit our witness. It is often right to differ from a person; it is always wrong to judge and criticize that person. "Judge not," said our Savior, "and you will not be judged."[4] The fact is that we cannot judge another without setting up ourselves as judges of human motive. Can we even judge correctly our own hearts with their hidden aspirations and desires and inborn deceitfulness? Then how much less another's! A human judge will view a case from every point of view before pronouncing judgment—and then is sometimes wrong. But we often pass cruel judgment on a fellow Christian knowing only one side of the case and little or nothing about the motives which lay behind his action.

We have no right to talk together about other people's weak points or sins unless it is done with the object of praying about them and being willing to go to the person concerned to face him with it in love. Let us never say anything about another behind his back that we would be unwilling to say to his face; and if we catch ourselves doing this let us go to the person concerned and apologize humbly. Let's all welcome the loving criticism of our friends (so different from condemnatory criticism) and ponder carefully what they say, not attempting to excuse ourselves and yet letting them know our point of view. If we are wrong, let's admit it fully and freely; if right, hold our ground humbly, but firmly.

"Do not reprove a scoffer, or he will hate you; reprove a wise man, and he will love you."[5] What a test of our spirituality is both the giving and receiving of such help! Where is this discipline of love among our ranks?

Lack of Self-Discipline Or again, how many of us can really be trusted to keep a confidence? How many of us pass things on "in confidence" simply because our tongues are undisciplined?

Moreover, if there is much negative conversation of the kind that is usually called *gossip,* there is also very little positive conversation of the kind that is usually called *witness.* The fact is that most of us make it the habit of our lives to witness neither to our fellow Christians nor to the outside world. We hide under the platitude, "It's the life that counts," when all the time the real reason for our silence is cowardice. We are afraid either to make ourselves or anyone else feel uncomfortable, with the result that nothing ever gets done.

A medical friend of mine made it the practice of his life to seek out someone each day to whom he could witness. He did not discriminate between converted and unconverted but simply passed on to anyone who would listen the glorious message of full salvation which he had proved, and was then proving, to be true. Such a discipline of love meant that he was ready and alert when a big opportunity came his way. And come his way it did. He became the spearhead of a revival that, starting at his mission hospital, swept through Central Africa and influenced the whole worldwide church. But unless the compelling power of such a discipline is the love of Christ—his dying love for the souls of men—the words become only jarring and meaningless noise.

May the love of Jesus fill me,
    As the waters fill the sea;

Him exalting, self abasing,
    This is victory.

May His beauty rest upon me
    As I seek the lost to win,
And may they forget the channel,
    Seeing only Him.

The Will and Its Choices

"... the good and acceptable and perfect will of God."[6]

"He must give up all right to himself, carry his cross every day and keep close behind me."[7]

How do we choose in life? What principles govern our actions? Most of us need to put into practice far more fully the principle of the cross, which is one of daily death to self and self-gratification. How often we choose the easier of two paths and therefore sometimes miss God's best for us. The harder path has the sharp pain of the cross in it, but also the glory of Easter morning. The easier has neither. This truth is at the heart of discipline. Everything else will fall into place if we are right here.

How do we spend our spare time? What we do with these minutes and hours shows what sort of people we are. Are we disciplined here? Are we God-controlled, "making the most of the time, because the days are evil"?[8]

Are we regular in answering our letters? Business-like in keeping our records? Orderly in our personal habits?

Do we ever discipline ourselves to silence after some solemn service or meeting to which we have been, so that we can get alone with God? Lack of this has meant loss of spiritual power with many of us.

Do we obey God's Word in checking each other's faults? "If a man is overtaken in any trespass, you who are spiritual should restore him in a spirit of gentleness. Look to yourself, lest you too be tempted."[9] Do we love one another sufficiently to risk being misunderstood in such an action? Are we bearing one another's burdens? We must recollect again and again that we are members of the same body, children of the same family, soldiers of the same army, and must move forward *together*. In this connection it is worth remembering that in some of the choices we shall have to make in working out this challenge in our lives there may be on our part a bias toward self-gratification. The story of Balaam in Numbers 22 is an example of this. An excellent guard against taking a wrong turning through the exceeding deceitfulness of the heart lies in finding out what an impartial friend thinks about it—one who is living the same type of life and will not be easy on us—and seriously taking into consideration what he says when weighing the situation before God.

The Mind and Its Thoughts

Our thoughts are molded largely by those things which enter our minds. It is, therefore, of vital importance to see that our mental food is chosen as carefully as our physical food. To assimilate mental poison is far more dangerous than to take physical poison because its presence is not so easily detected or eliminated, and its effects are more insidiously harmful and often less obnoxious. How important it is to choose correctly and adamantly refuse anything less than the best!

What sort of books do we read? Quite apart from the poor and indifferent ones (and not to mention those that are suggestive or unhealthy), there are so many good ones that we must choose carefully between even these. Enlightened conscience decides between good and evil; God's guidance between good and good. Are we guided in what we read?

Then there are our studies. Some students read solely with the objective of passing exams. Is this an adequate motive? Let's remember that all work is God's work and must be done for his glory. If there is anything we cannot call his, it would be better dropped. Are we methodical or haphazard in our reading? Much of our parents' time and money and of God's time and money is wasted through lack of method, while we proceed to become progressively less efficient. Do wandering thoughts and daydreams fritter away our time? I have found that one minute of prayer preceding an hour's work does miracles in keeping the mind concentrated because the work is now conscientiously being done for the Lord Jesus.

Are we doing a *real* day's work? Six days shalt

thou *work*.

Are we disciplined in our reading of the Bible?[10] I discovered only recently that my study of the Bible was inadequate. I had allowed the urgent duties of Christian service to crowd out any sustained and deep study. This had to be remedied at once. Besides this, God may want us to memorize at least one verse from his Word each day. Have you ever tried memorizing an important chapter or Epistle?

What sort of pictures do we look at? These are sometimes hung on the walls of the imagination and play a large part in determining the kind of life we live. "Sow a thought, reap an act; sow an act, reap a habit; sow a habit, reap a character; sow a character, reap a *destiny*." All deliberate sin starts in the mind. What sort of shop windows and people do we notice? Do certain TV programs or advertisements leave a mental sediment? Let's settle definitely in our minds which things we habitually see are good and which are less than good, and then let's discipline ourselves deliberately to cultivate the best and avoid the others.

What conversations do we listen to? One conversation entered upon by a keen university man lately made wholesome thoughts more difficult for weeks afterwards. He would prefer an attack of colic any day, he said! "We are not what we think we are, but what we *think*—we *are*."

"Fix your minds on the things that are holy and right and pure and beautiful and good."[11]

"Take every thought captive to obey Christ."[12]

The Heart and Its Emotions

This has been touched upon in the chapter on love, and it only needs to be added here that some of us tend to be undisciplined and selfish in the realm of religious emotion. Those of us who are demonstrative forget that others equally sincere and wholehearted in their faith and loyalty to Christ find it difficult to pray and worship with us because we seem to intrude *ourselves* into the picture, unconscious that our action has taken other people's thoughts away from God. Sometimes, too, we sing the words of a hymn or chorus in the same way that a man of the world sings his jazz, and evidently with much the same end in view—that is, being happy and cheerful with others of the same spirit. This sometimes verges on blasphemy. We would do far better with some decent secular songs. Those who are less demonstrative, however, need equally to appreciate the point of view and feelings of the other. "Humbly considering each other the better man," writes Paul.[13]

The Body and Its Instincts

Sleep Are we disciplined with regard to sleep—the time we go to bed? the time we get up? Who is master —ourselves or our body? Some of us are lazy, others ascetic; do we treat our bodies as the temples of the Holy Spirit? It would seem sensible to decide how many hours' sleep we need in order to be at our best physically, and then to be disciplined enough to take those hours—no more, no less. Of course, there are exceptions, but have we a rule? Some say they have a rule, but actually it proves to be far more an exception. This is the opposite of discipline—"A house divided against itself. . . ."

Some of us do not get up in the morning for an adequate quiet time with God because we do not go to bed at night sufficiently early. We need to brave the possibility of being misunderstood and called unsociable, and simply say "Goodnight," whatever is happening, and go to bed. If we explain why we are going, the majority of people will understand; but even if they do not, better that than disappointing Christ. Nothing in the day is of greater importance than our meeting with him in the early morning. Let's not be too tired to give him time at night, too—if necessary doing so early in the evening and later on just saying a reverent and loving "Good night, Lord Jesus," before getting into bed.

Food Do we eat in moderation? Some of us eat until we can't comfortably eat any more and then stop. This is what the animals do. I know of at least one unconverted student who was put off from coming to Christ by the gluttony of a Christian. In this connection, it is worthwhile educating our tastes and appetites by deliberately eating from time to time what we do not like,[14] and at other times by stopping before we are completely satisfied. This might be done regularly several times a week.

Do we ever fast? Evangelicals in reaction against the false asceticism of certain forms of Christianity have tended to put very little emphasis on fasting, and this has been to their detriment. What little has been done in this direction during the season of Lent in most families has been a farce. It has even been the fashion to spiritualize away some of the plain statements of the New Testament about it and to regard it with suspicion when practiced by others. The person who takes Christ seriously on this matter is thought of as either a religious fanatic or an extreme High Churchman!

From the medical point of view the missing of, say, one meal per week, would do many people a great deal of good. One can say, with small chance of contradiction by a medical authority, that most people habitually eat too much. On the other hand, of course, some eat too little, and although they would still be among the majority who would be helped physically by regular fasting, they should also eat more and better food (where possible) at their regular meals.

Mr. Hoste, a former Director of the China Inland Mission, once wrote home suggesting that this generation of Christians was not being taught to fast and was missing very much as a result. Many of us know that he missed breakfast twice each week in order to spend more time in prayer; and he was one of the busiest men in China!

When we fast, let us do it secretly (unless this is impossible) so that our motive may be pure and spiritual. Our fast is to God.[15]

Recreation Prowess in sports, if consecrated, is

often of great value in Christ's service as well as in
building up a fit body—the sanctuary of his indwelling Spirit. Whatever we take up let us do it with all
our might. Let's beware of lesser motives or of allowing sports to become an idol. Writing in the *Inter-Varsity Magazine*, an old Cambridge Blue says, "Looking
back on the sport side of my life, I think it is here I find
the greatest regrets. It occupied too prominent a place
until the finger of God pointed out the idol. May I
give an example? During my second year at Cambridge, by most of the people interested I was thought
to be a certainty for the Varsity athletic side. I had
lived and prayed for this, yet when the day of the
sports came—results were different. What a crash it
was! It seemed as though life was hardly worth living
until, once again face to face with Christ, I had to acknowledge sport had pushed Him out of first place.
Oh! the peace of learning the secret of the words given
to me by a friend who had had success at that time:

He knows, He loves, He cares;

   Nothing this truth can dim;

He gives the very best to those

   Who leave the choice to Him.

"Since that time I have never prayed for success
at sport, but only that I may glorify Him, whether in
success or failure, knowing that 'my disappointments
are His appointments.' This has in no way dimin-
ished my keenness or ardor, but rather increased it for
His glory."

Another sportsman, an international Rugby foot-

ball player living in the South of England, is known to
have given up Rugby for a whole season to be able to
play soccer with the young fellows of his church
whom he wished to win for Christ.

Most of us are not great sportsmen, however, and
some of us may be failing to treat our bodies as the
sanctuaries of the Holy Spirit. Are we getting enough
regular exercise? Quantity in work can never make up
for lack of quality, and no person can do his best work
with an overtired body. Do we get fresh air regularly?
Do we do physical exercises each morning and have a
cold bath?

Conclusion

Robert Wilder says in his delightful little book, *Christ
and the Student World*, "One should study himself and
see where he is weak, and double the sentries at that
point. In India I visited a fort which was five and a
quarter miles in circumference and very strong. There
was one weak point in the fortification, however, and
through that point the enemy entered one dark night
and captured the fort. *Now* at that point there is a tri-
ple defence, and it has been made the most carefully
guarded, as well as the strongest part of the fortification. That is wisdom. Are we as wise?"

Let's not fall into the trap of attempting to complete
by "the works of the flesh" what has been started in
us by "the faith of Christ." That was the mistake the
Galatians made which called forth Paul's Epistle to
them. "Are you so foolish?" he writes. "Having be-

gun with the Spirit, are you now ending with the flesh?''[16] Both justification and sanctification are by faith and faith alone—the free gift of God—but this fullness of life given to us by God is utilized to the best advantage and given room to expand, grow and bear fruit only as we tread the path of discipline and sacrifice.[17] Peter, too, makes it abundantly clear that it is our responsibility to add to our faith self-control.[18] Let us then do it.

"Every competitor in athletic events goes into serious training," writes Paul. Athletes will take tremendous pains—for a fading crown of leaves. But our contest is for an eternal trophy that will never fade.

"I run the race then with determination. I am no shadow-boxer, I really fight! I am my body's sternest master, for fear that when I have preached to others I should myself be disqualified."[19]

EXPERIENCE

"TO ME, THOUGH I AM THE VERY LEAST OF ALL THE SAINTS, THIS GRACE WAS GIVEN, TO PREACH TO THE GENTILES THE UNSEARCHABLE RICHES OF CHRIST."[1]

Our Christian experiences differ in their details but agree in certain central truths. All, too, unite in Christ. If the following narrative serves to reemphasize certain of those truths and, above all, to bring glory to our Lord and Savior, it will have justified its inclusion in this volume. I am, however, somewhat hesitant about allowing it to appear, but, knowing that God has used it when spoken to help some to a simpler faith and to a more wholehearted surrender to Christ, I feel that God may be able to use it in its written form to that same end. It is told as frankly as possible and with an honest attempt to exclude either overstatement or cowardice.

A Christian Home

I can never repay the debt I owe to my parents for the dedicated Christian home in which I was brought up. My father was a qualified doctor who never practiced because of the demands of full-time church work. He was a missionary leader, an evangelist and a lecturer for the Y.M.C.A. He owed much of his vision to his father, Henry Grattan Guinness, who drew tens of thousands to hear the gospel when he and Spurgeon were young men together. My mother was quiet, determined and practical, which was just as well since she was married to my father!

When I was eleven my father died and, as I wept at his open grave, God came very close to me. This was to bear fruit three years later in my conversion.

Conversion

My mother and five of the nine children (four boys and a girl) moved from the huge rambling house at Sydenham, England, to a much smaller house at Upper Norwood where we would be near Christ Church, Gipsy Hill. Mr. Green, father of Canon Bryan Green, was in charge of the Boy Crusaders' Bible Class which met each Sunday afternoon.

It was through this class that I found Christ. Its ringleaders were Max Warren, Bryan Green, Roger de Pemberton and my brother Gordon, and relentlessly they pursued me (as well as many other boys) until I was finally won. The climax came one Saturday evening when Bryan Green invited me to a prayer meeting and spoke to me about my need of accepting Christ personally. "Have you ever said 'thank you' to Christ," he said, "for dying for you on the cross?" I never had and told him so. "Won't you?" he insisted. It was then that God revealed to me my sin and my Savior. My ingratitude seemed to me to be the worst of sins—worse than my dishonesties, temper or selfishness. Indeed it seemed to me in the light of Christ's cross a very damnable thing. What worse is there than indifference in the face of such love?

"Thank You, Lord Jesus, for dying for me," I prayed. "Take my life. You can do anything you want with it."

And he took me at my word. He stepped right into the center of my life and brought to me the peace of forgiveness and the joy of his companionship. At last my Christian faith, received from my parents and watered by their many prayers, had come alive. Christ was mine and I was his.

The same week I told some of my friends. The same year I was baptized and confirmed.

Witness

At the Leys, Cambridge, where my brother Gordon and I went the following year, we set about forming a prayer meeting. The chaplain, Conrad Skinner, loaned us his room and with his good will we met for ten minutes each lunch hour. There must have been half a dozen of us meeting quite soon and we took turns reading a passage of Scripture, explaining it if we could and leading in prayer. Others would then pray as they felt able and when the last prayer had been uttered we would rise from our knees.

We suffered a certain amount of persecution for this (how could it have been otherwise at a boarding school?), but it did us good; and we know that it was worth it, too, from the spiritual results in the lives of some of the other boys.

Unfortunately we were not very consistent Christians, and I fell into many sins I regret. But despite this God seemed to work, and the meeting grew and prospered. In the holidays we began to attend the University and Public School Camps, and later to work with the CSSM (Children's Sand and Surf Mission). My first seaside mission was at Bude, Cornwall, where Gordon (aged 21) was the leader. All the rest of the team from Cambridge and London were younger still. I believe good work was done despite our youth, and maybe because of it.

Freedom

After four years of typical school life I entered St. Bartholomew's Hospital, London, with a Christian reputation but little else. It was while there that the Holy Spirit brought me through a number of crises which lifted me on to successively higher levels of service and freedom. To me they have been the "crises of sanctification."

The first came at the end of my first year. I was becoming utterly dissatisfied with my Christian experi-

ence and attainment. Here I was, an open and acknowledged Christian who was doing Sunday school
work, camp work, CSSM work, Inter-Varsity work,
slum work and a Bible correspondence course, and yet
was defeated in the inner recess of my own moral
being by such things as dishonesty and impurity,
which together with the lack of time found for private
prayer, left me powerless to lead others to the Savior. I
longed to help others. It was at this time that I decided
to apply to a certain missionary society for work
abroad, and yet I was so proud that, rather than acknowledge myself unfit for the task, I deceived myself
into telling a lie. It was easy enough to answer the
questions on doctrine, but not so easy to answer one
that dealt with experience. "Have you reason to believe," read the question, "that you have been the
means of leading another to know Christ as Savior?" I
scratched my head. Yes, surely I had. It simply meant
bringing one of the many to memory. Let me think.
And I thought! But think as I might none of the
"many" came to mind, and I was forced on to the very
thin ice of selecting as an illustration a boy who had
been brought by me to a meeting, who had been in-
troduced to the speaker afterwards and who, as a result, I thought, had been converted. And, as I wrote,
my conscience was almost happy, such is the deceitfulness of sin. My standard of honesty was not very
high, for I was more concerned about my reputation
than anything else. But the consideration of that question, with the resultant realization of my comparative

uselessness, made me long all the more to be used really effectively by God and drove me tc my knees one night. What was keeping me back from a life of power in his service? Almost immediately two things emerged from the chaos of my thoughts: (1) I was a slave to a besetting sin which made me despise myself and (2) I was giving God no time and taking no orders from him at the start of each day. I was running my own life.

And so the Holy Spirit brought me to my second great inclusive surrender to Christ since the day I first trusted him five years before. It was inclusive because every fibre of my being went into it. It was not vague, for it centered in the morning "quiet time" and a willingness to get out of bed at least half an hour earlier than was my habit to meet with God. If I remember my prayer correctly, it was something like this: "Lord, if you will rid me of this rotten habit which has enslaved me, I will do anything you like." He took me at my word, for out it went, and with a new-found freedom, a new sense of direction, and a new and thrilling joy in his unseen presence. I flung myself into the work of winning my fellow students for my Lord and Savior.

Power for Service

The second crisis came in my third year. My progress in evangelism had been slow as far as my hospital friends were concerned, and, although I had the joy of winning a number of schoolboys at camp and seaside missions, no one of my own age had yet professed conversion through my witness. I was getting a little discouraged, and the rapid approach of further exams was making me a little slack in the morning "quiet times." It was difficult to work into the early hours of the morning and also be up before breakfast for prayer. Moreover, sports added to the difficulty, for it was impossible for me to cut down my hours of sleep in view of the need of being fit enough for Club Rugby Football as well. This time God spoke to me through a book on prayer which I was reading while traveling south with the rest of the hospital team toward Portsmouth. It was Payne's *The Greatest Force on Earth*, and I was so impressed that I wrote in the flyleaf, "From today the central thing in my life shall be prayer." To put this resolution into force meant revolution. The whole of my life would need reorganization, but I knew it would be worth it whatever the cost because of Christ's promise, "Seek ye first the kingdom of God, and his righteousness, and all these things [including academic attainment] shall be added unto you."[2] What I did immediately was to decide how many hours' sleep I needed and work back from the hour at which I wished to rise to fix the time at which I must close up my books and go to bed. The habit of my life, as a student, from that day on was to go to bed at the hour thus fixed, unless something of pressing urgency kept me.

What a change! What an eagerly anticipated hour was that first hour of the day, and what resplendent glories were revealed to my soul! What treasures were discovered in his Word, and unspeakable joys made mine through prayer! No words can express the sacredness of those experiences when I met my God face to face and held communion with him.

The result in my life gradually became evident to everyone. I found myself whistling and singing with joy wherever I went, so great was the exhilaration and joy of living. Daily witnessing to those I met on my way to the hospital and home again kept that song exultant. This was life indeed! And as though to crown my new and abundant joy I had the thrill of leading to Christ a week later a young businessman of my own age with whom I was traveling to town. My Savior was beginning to fulfill his promise of the "rivers of living water" which were to flow from the believing soul. He was beginning to make a weak and sinful creature a "fisher of men." Thanks be to God.

Humility

The third crisis came in my fourth year of medicine. I had become the vice-chairman of the recently formed Inter-Varsity Fellowship and was attending one of their annual conferences at High Leigh. It was the evening meeting, and the subject was the cross of our Lord Jesus Christ. It was very solemn. We were in the very presence of the Lamb of God who bore the sin of the world. We saw him suffer, we heard him cry out in desolation, we beheld him die, and bowed at his pierced feet. Through it all one cry haunted me and would not let me go. It was read to us from Psalm 22, the thoughts of which could only be the Spirit of Christ speaking through the prophet and foretelling his sufferings[3] because of verses 16, 17 and 18, which describe so minutely the death by crucifixion in a day when it was unknown. That haunting cry was in verse 6: "I am a worm and no man." The Son of God had not merely been born of a woman, but in a stable; had not merely died, but been nailed to a cross; had not merely been nailed to a cross, but between two murderers; had not merely died between two murderers an outcast from man, *but an outcast from God.* He who knew no sin had *become* sin for us, that we might be made the righteousness of God in him. The Son of God had not merely become man, but, in stooping to where we lay (wounded by sin and dying) had become a "worm" among men. Was it possible? The thought staggered me and left me marveling at this mighty humbling which only Deity could have conceived. Then came the challenge. Had I ever taken the place of a "worm"? Had I ever acknowledged myself to be nothing before God? Was I in my Christian experience thinking of myself as one superior to other people, especially to those of other classes and nations for whom Christ also died? Did he come down to one level to pick me up and then go further down so as to include them? If I had marveled that Christ became a worm for us men, I also began now to marvel at the implication that faced me and forced itself upon me— I also was a worm.

I a worm? Nothing was further from my thoughts. I had a most unusual and happy combination of gifts which (to my mind) made me a person much to be desired. Was I vice-chairman of the Conference for nothing? Had I been elected president of the Hospital Christian Union by chance? Wasn't my athletic record one to be proud of and my popularity at the hospital a thing to draw attention to the fact of what a likeable fellow I must be? Wasn't I a gifted person with much to be thankful to God for, and could I not rightly pray with humility and restraint, "Lord, I thank thee I am not as other men"? Without being boastful and proud, wasn't I a cut above most?

A worm.

This conclusion was forced upon me by the very power of that degrading death and outpoured blood. The house of cards came tumbling about my ears; my accomplishments were nothing; all my righteousness (the very cream of life) but filthy rags—a beggar's vermin-infested clouts! My soul was in actual fact stripped and naked before the searching tribunal of God as never before.

The meeting was ending and prayer was being offered. Our heads and hearts were bowed in the deepest solemnity, when suddenly I was brought up short and began to perspire. What was the speaker saying? "I want those who have never before taken the place of worms before God to acknowledge that fact and take that position now by standing in their places." I might have fled from the place could I have done so, but it was impossible; I was wedged in tightly. It was one thing to acknowledge a fact before God, but quite another thing to do so before men. How humiliating it would be to admit that I who was looked up to so much for Christian character, was anything less than that which they had thought me! So the battle raged for perhaps three minutes, before pride—that cursed desire to be thought well of by others—gave way before the power of Christ's cross. I stood.

I do not remember any vast change in my outward life as a result of that confession, but I know that a new humility began to take possession of me and that on the wall of my room went up the inscription, *"I am a worm!"* Many a time since then pride has reared its ugly head—although wounded to death—and thought to woo and win me into friendship (and at times, alas! has temporarily succeeded), but the cross has always conquered in the end, the spiritual sin been revealed, repented of, confessed and cleansed away in the precious blood of Christ. "Thanks be to God, who gives us the victory through our Lord Jesus Christ."[4]

Frequent Adjustments
Other smaller needs for readjustment are always meeting me as I tread this narrow and glorious path. The challenge of the Oxford groups faced me with the fact that I was not being really loving in my human relationships and was thereby letting Christ down badly. I had not written to, or seen, a sister of mine in

England for five years. I will not excuse myself by saying that I came from a family of nine, and two of those years had been spend abroad, because that leaves three perfectly respectable years in which to perform the brotherly and not very costly act of writing a letter. Of course, I wrote at once to apologize and went to see her within a month. She was delighted!

Or again, I tended to be careless about the small things of life and not to carry Christ into certain things which I had decided did not matter. Tidiness was one of these. I decided I had been born untidy and that it was not the sort of thing Christ worried about anyway, so I could put it out of my mind. It never occurred to me that someone else had to pick up the things I left lying around. Answering important letters promptly was another of these, and failing to return things "borrowed" was another. For instance, while writing some notes on "restitution" in Australia, May, 1934, I found that in my bags and trunks I had eight separate articles which belonged to various people with whom I stayed in England and elsewhere. I had not deliberately taken them; I had just not bothered about the smaller things and had put off sending back the others. Needless to say a number of letters of apology had to be written that night although I was packing to leave the next day and it was late. The Holy Spirit has driven me to see that the little things matter intensely, for Christ is judged in us by the little things we do or omit to do.

"I have been crucified with Christ; it is no longer I

who live, but Christ who lives in me; and the life I now live in the flesh I live by faith in the Son of God, who loved me and gave himself for me."[5]

The Greatest Test of All

Twenty-four years have gone by and again I put pen to paper. Each year has confirmed me in the love of Christ and the power of the gospel to save sinful men and women. And I have come to love and trust our glorious Savior more than ever. In middle age there comes that insidious temptation to settle down and to come to terms with little sins. I have faced this and know it for the reality it is. I have sometimes won and sometimes lost in the battle, and my opinion of myself is nothing to write home about. As a result, when I preach on sanctification there is never any danger of my teaching being interpreted as "sinless perfection," although I have reason to know that the imperative call to holy (Christ-like) living is clearly heard. My own experience makes certain of that.

But there is one thing I say endlessly and tirelessly and joyously about myself. It is this:

O Saviour, I have naught to plead,
    In earth beneath or heaven above,
Save only my exceeding need,
    And Thy exceeding love.

During the last eleven years my family and I have lived in Australia. How generously the Australian IVF welcomed us here in 1949! How good it was to meet old friends again—Howard Mowll, T. C. Hammond, J. B. Nicholson, Paul White and a host of others. Before we had settled into St. Barnabas' Rectory I was speaking to the Inter-Varsity Annual Conference at Castlereagh on "Launch Out into the Deep," and enjoying the unique experience of hearing about forty of them render parts of the Messiah most movingly under Bill Andersen's able leadership.

Then followed an endless round of activity and joyous service for ten years, seven of them at St. Barnabas' and three at St. Michael's. Our home became a center for the Evangelical Union and as a result a ceaseless procession of undergraduates from the university across the road entered our home for study groups, personal advice, prayer or romps with the children. At one time so many cups of tea were consumed each week that I got into hot water with my wife over it!

Missions to all the universities of Australasia were arranged with the exception of Tasmania. My wife and I flew twice to New Zealand and came to love that land and its charming people.

A monthly university service was begun at St. Barnabas' Church, and from time to time the "devil's advocate" method was used when the case against Christianity was presented before the gospel was preached. On the whole this method stimulated real thought and is therefore to be commended.

Added to this was writing and publishing work, the St. Andrew's Cathedral Wednesday Mid-day Service, the School's Forum of the Air, social work, and the rebuilding of our Church premises (Broadway Community Center).

Throughout this decade, during which God most graciously allowed me to see many souls won for Christ's kingdom and go out as witnesses into the world, I was fighting a losing battle with my voice. It gradually lost more and more of its resonance, despite all that doctors and voice specialists could do for it, until finally I gave up the agonizing struggle and early this year asked my church council for leave from parish duties for six months. Nine months have now gone by and still there is no improvement, although the best advice has been sought and much prayer has surrounded me.

A tough test!

God, I often think, is very brave! But there is no resentment. (How could there be?) Our Father is much too loving to be unkind, and much too wise to make a mistake.

As a result of my illness, my wife, who had picked up the load I had been forced to drop and carried it at a cost known only to herself, collapsed and was forced to spend several weeks in bed and many more recuperating. Thus the test was toughened more. I was frankly puzzled but not cast down, for I had long since learned to trust where I could not understand. The Lord still reigned! And help from many friends (not least our own children) surrounded us so wonderfully that in the end we blessed the Lord for his mercies and took courage.

Then out of the blue several enlarged glands appeared in different parts of my body, and my doctor looked anxious as he examined me. When he had finished, he said frankly, "You ought to know the truth. This is probably either Hodgkin's disease or lymphosarcoma. We will know when we have had a look at one of the glands."

Before the biopsy (surgical removal of the gland for examination) was done, I had read up on the subject and knew that either diagnosis was a sentence of death—a somewhat slow and unpleasant one that would take anywhere up to ten years and, in certain circumstances, a longer time. All treatment was palliative. After the biopsy I knew that the diagnosis was lymphosarcoma.

The final test had come. God was braver than ever! Could I trust him fully now?

When the first nightmarish mist had cleared from my eyes I saw to my astonishment the glory of the Lord shining upon me. In all his wonder and beauty and love he had burst upon my soul and filled me to overflowing with himself. The final test had become a great privilege, the "unthinkable" an opportunity of witness, the end the BEGINNING! Each day I found myself rejoicing in *life* and full of thankfulness. The day after the operation they had to let me go home because I was so full of radiant and overflowing health. Neither doctor nor nurse could hold me!

And yet my race is nearing its end. Unless God intervenes directly (and I am wide open to his loving administrations of healing if he wills life) it looks as though I have entered the home stretch, and it is now or never for that final effort.

I never stood a chance of running a four-minute mile. My time will be a very ordinary one, I fear. But it has been the best I could manage. If I were to run the race again, I imagine there would be no significant speeding up of the lap times, although I hope I would stumble less when jostled by the other runners and give way more graciously when they passed me.

But this last lap: *I would love it to be the best of all.* Can I summon all my energies for one last supreme effort, and, refusing to believe the evidence of those aching muscles and dragging feet, hurl myself towards the tape to break it—a gallant runner at least, if not a good one? I must. For at the tape stands none other than the Judge himself, and all around in the great unseen arena are the spectators in their billions —"the great cloud of witnesses"—who are already raising the thunderous shout of encouragement which is spurring me to the supreme effort of my life.

POWER

"ALL POWER... HAS BEEN GIVEN TO ME."[1]
□ "WE HAVE THIS TREASURE IN EARTHEN VES-
SELS, TO SHOW THAT THE TRANSCENDENT
POWER BELONGS TO GOD AND NOT TO US."[2]
"You shall receive power when the Holy Spirit has
come upon you; and you shall be my witnesses... to
the end of the earth."[3] It was the risen Savior who
thus spoke, and the power given at Pentecost revolu-
tionized the disciples, the pagan empire of Rome and
the whole subsequent course of civilization.

"The real power," says Spurgeon, "lies in the out-
going of the Godhead, in the majesty of the Eternal
Might upon the hearts and consciences of men. It is
the *Holy Ghost* and the power of *Jesus Himself* that
must accomplish the deed." He proved it in his own
life, and thousands of men before and since, in their
own sphere, have proved it true as well. Indeed, this
New Testament Christianity is being rediscovered

by hundreds of normal and intelligent people in this modern age nineteen hundred years after the Holy Spirit was given at Pentecost. Let's examine what the Bible has to say on this subject, supplementing the passages quoted with others suggested in the notes or obtainable from any Bible concordance.

The Prophets "A new heart I will give you, and a new spirit I will put within you . . . and I will put *my spirit* within you, and cause you to walk in my statutes . . . and I will deliver you from *all* uncleannesses. . . ."[4]

Christ's Forerunner "I baptize you with water for repentance . . . he will baptize you with the Holy Spirit and with fire."[5]

Christ Himself "If any one thirst, let him come to me and drink. He who believes in me, as the Scripture has said, 'out of his heart shall flow rivers of living water.' Now this he said about the Spirit."[6]

The Apostle Paul "Do you not know that your body is a temple of the Holy Spirit within you, which you have from God? You are not your own."[7]

These represent only a fraction of the promises of God about the Holy Spirit which form the warp and woof of the New Testament and of which the apostle says, "Every promise of God finds its affirmative in him, and through him can be said the final amen, to the glory of God."[8] These promises are ours and cover all the various needs of our individual lives if only we will search them out, claim them by faith, do the will of God and receive them as our own.[9] They open up heaven on earth for us.

The whole question of being filled with the Holy Spirit has been made very complicated by various Christian groups. A flood of light entered my mind and soul once at the Keswick Convention when a speaker, commenting on the muddle that exists in people's minds on the subject, said words something like these: "God is One and indivisible. When I receive Christ in conversion I receive therefore the Holy Spirit. And further, when I enthrone Christ I receive the fullness of the Holy Spirit, for he is now free to do what he wills with me." How simple it all became:

Receive Christ... receive the Holy Spirit.

Enthrone Christ... receive the fullness of the Holy Spirit.

When I receive Christ as my Savior, the attitude of my heart and will must be that of simple trust and unconditional surrender. Nothing less than this swings wide the door for him to enter, for he is a *King*. Failure to realize this sometimes leads to false conversions and subsequent falling away. At the moment of conversion, therefore, Christ is not only received but enthroned, and I am "filled with the Holy Spirit." There is no reason why I should not progress in the life of this fullness right from that moment, but the fact is that most of us fail to do so through disobedience or unbelief, with the result that Christ is dethroned and "self" takes his place. He does not leave us at such moments, however,[10] but waits sorrowfully for us to see our mistake and return to him in penitence and surrender. With many of us there comes a

conscious time—or period of time—sometimes after
we have been defeated Christians for several years
when we re-enthrone the Savior and are freed from
self and sin by the inflooding power of the Holy Spirit.

There is one vital difference between these parallel
truths of receiving and enthroning Christ, however.
The first is done once for all and I become "born of
God."[11] The second is not done once for all, but is a
moment-by-moment experience which, started by a
definite act, and at first continued by many similar
acts, finally becomes habitual through the settled attitude of my will. Many acts lead on to a constant attitude. A crisis starts a process. This does not secure
for us "sinless perfection"[12]—the inability to sin. But
it does secure freedom—the ability not to sin.

A letter lies in front of me which shows the way into
this experience. It comes from a university man who
lately has trodden that path and is on fire to pass on
the message. Here is its outline. I have filled it in and
added to it in certain places.

How to Prepare for this Fuller Experience

1. Let us try to realize as fully as we can that our
sins and ineffectiveness hurt the One we love. If it is
true that we are pained when we see those we love
dearly falling below the high ideals we have set them
and living lives of selfishness and self-indulgence,
how much more our Savior when he looks upon us! Our
supreme motive, therefore, for seeking this fuller experience should be Christ's love for us. "The love of

Christ controls us."[13]

2. Let us surrender ourselves utterly to the incoming and overmastering power and love of the Holy Spirit. This should not only be the act of a moment, but also the act, often repeated, of a will which wants to make absolutely sure that it is abandoned to God's will. It is a life of moment-by-moment surrender to search out diligently the will of God and to obey it.

3. Let us repent fully of sins committed against other people and put right, to the utmost of our ability, what may be wrong between ourselves and them.[14] Let us make all the adjustments that need to be made for this new life regardless of cost where we are concerned and in the spirit of love where others are concerned.

4. Let us be desperately concerned about the whole thing. Those who *hunger* and *thirst* for righteousness shall be filled.[15] But we must come to an end of ourselves—our prayers, our earnestness, our knowledge of the Bible, our witnessing, our Christian work, our attainments, our past experience, *our* anything—and thus start to know the true death of self and union with the Crucified.[16] We must despair of ourselves[17] and consent to the fact that our sinful nature was nailed to the cross with Christ nineteen hundred years ago,[18] thus, potentially, liberating us from its thralldom and power.

The Miracle Itself
By faith we must fling out our challenge to God to be

faithful to his promises. For he has promised to deliver us now,[19] to fill us with his Holy Spirit[20] and to keep us forever.[21] Is he not faithful who has promised?[22] Let us then risk everything on him. Let us come in faith and abandonment and cast our lives on God's faithfulness and love. Then, and then only, will we be able to read A. B. Simpson's wonderful words and rejoice in them because they are indeed true of us:

> I take salvation full and free,
> Thro' Him Who gave His life for me.
> He undertakes my all to be.
>> I take—He undertakes.

> I take the promised Holy Ghost,
> I take the power of Pentecost,
> To fill me to the uttermost.
>> I take—He undertakes.

> I simply take Him at His word,
> I praise Him that my prayer is heard,
> And claim my answer from the Lord.
>> I take—He undertakes.

> I take Thee, blessed Lord,
> I give myself to Thee,
> And Thou, according to Thy word
>> Dost undertake for me.

EPILOGUE

It occurred during one of the early offensives of World War I. The Australians were experimenting with mines, and it was of sufficient importance for the Brigadier-General to come up to the front line trenches to make observations for himself. Among other things, his job was to press the button which would connect the circuit and blow up the mine. The advance was timed for zero hour—dawn on a cold November day.

All was in readiness. The sappers had done their work well, and the mine chamber was filled with TNT, the highest explosive then known. The men were buckling on their accoutrements, seeing to their bayonets and drinking their grog in silence. It was the darkest hour preceding dawn, and nerves were on edge. Some were praying. And then just the faintest suspicion of light tinged the sky, and the black of night was beginning to give way to the grey of early morning. There was still five minutes to go. A whispered warning went flying down the trench. The Brigadier in the dugout looked at his watch and compared it with the Major's. They nodded assent. The hour had come. He deliberately pressed the button.

Nothing happened.

It was a moment of acute crisis. The men were almost immediately going over the top, mine or no mine, and the enemy's position was bristling with machine-guns. They might take it, but at tremendous cost of life. Just at that moment the Sapper Lieutenant, who had been standing by, turned to the Brigadier and said, "Excuse me, sir, but I think I know what's wrong." And in a moment he had disappeared through the doorway and down the tunnel leading to the mine. The moments seemed as hours to those two as they stood there tense and straining, with the perspiration standing out on their foreheads—waiting. A minute had passed. And then an ear-splitting and deafening roar told its own tale, the air became filled with smoke and dust and falling debris, and the men were already halfway across no-man's-land at a steady run. There was little resistance, the position was soon theirs, and they began setting about the work of consolidation. *But the Sapper Lieutenant was not seen again.* He had had to decide in a fraction of a second whether he would die or they; he had faced death for sixty seconds pushing his way through the mine tunnel and had died the death of a gallant gentleman in the chamber itself.

Where are the young men and women of this generation who will hold their lives cheap,[1] and be faithful even unto death? Where are those who will lose their lives for Christ's sake—flinging them away for love of him? Where are those who will live dangerously and be reckless in his service?[2] Where are his *lovers* —those who love him and the souls of men more than their own reputations or comfort, or very life?

Where are the men who say "no" to self; who take up Christ's cross to bear it after him; who are willing to be nailed to it in college or office, home or mission field; who are willing, if need be, to bleed, to suffer and to die on it?

Where are the men of vision today? Where are the men of enduring vision? Where are the men who have seen the King in his beauty, by whom from henceforth all else is counted but refuse that they may win Christ? Where are the adventurers, the explorers, the pioneers for God who count one human soul of far greater value than the rise or fall of an empire? Where are the men of glory in God-sent loneliness, difficulties, persecutions, misunderstandings, discipline, sacrifice, death?

Where are the men who are willing to pay the price of vision?

Where are the men of prayer? Where are the men who, like the psalmist of old, count God's Word of more importance to them than their daily food? Where are the men who, like Moses, commune with God face to face as a man speaks with his friend, and unmistakably bear with them the fragrance of the meeting through the day?

Where are God's men in this day of God's power?

Notes

Chapter 1

[1]Mt. 5:3.

[2]Lk. 14:33.

[3]Phil. 2:7.

[4]Heb. 2:11.

[5]"Inasmuch as ye have done it unto the least of these my brethren, ye have done it unto me" (Mt. 25:40, AV).

[6]Heb. 10:34.

[7]Mt. 5:3, "Poor in spirit"; one poor by choice; one who has renounced his right to everything the world has to offer, so that anything which comes to him is pure gain and is accepted as God's good gift. If things which others prize do not come to him, they are not feverishly sought after, whether they be money, property, reputation, loved ones, health or even life itself.

[8]Mk. 12:42-44.

[9]1 Cor. 10:23.

[10]1 Cor. 8:9.

[11]C. E. Padwick, *Temple Gairdner of Cairo*, p. 53.

[12]For further help on this subject see Yvonne Vinkemulder's challenging booklet, *Enrich Your Life* (IVP).

[13]Mt. 5:3.

Chapter 2

[1] Jn. 15:13.
[2] Jn. 21:15.
[3] Jn. 1:12.
[4] 1 Cor. 13:4-8 (J. B. Phillips).
[5] Eph. 2:1.
[6] Eph. 3:17-19.
[7] Herbert Gray, *Men, Women and God*, p. 32.
[8] Bryan Green, *Problems of Human Friendship*.
[9] Gray, *Men, Women and God*, p. 49.
[10] Ibid., pp. 18 and 20.
[11] This is becoming far less common.
[12] Lutterworth Press and China Inland Mission.
[13] Mt. 7:14.
[14] Song 2:7; 3:5; 8:4.
[15] G. Campbell Morgan, *Living Messages*, p. 80.
[16] McDougall: "The grand word, integrity, most adequately describes the perfectly healthy personality, the man ... in whom discipline and self-discipline have built up, from a native basis of disposition, temperament and character. All functional disorders of the repressive type imply failure to maintain integrity."
[17] L. D. Weatherhead, *Psychology and Life*, p. 124.
[18] 1 Cor. 8:11-13.
[19] Green, *Problems of Human Friendship*.
[20] Rom. 1:1; Phil. 1:1.
[21] 1 Tim. 6:8.
[22] Phil. 4:11.
[23] Mt. 6:33.
[24] See A. N. Triton, *Living and Loving* (IVP), and C. Stephen Board, *HIS Guide to Sex, Singleness and Marriage* (IVP).
[25] Rom. 12:1-2.

Chapter 3

[1] See Prov. 4:13: Hebrew *mussar*.
[2] S.C.M., 1926.

[3]Mt. 23:3.
[4]Lk. 6:37.
[5]Prov. 9:8.
[6]Rom. 12:2 (RSV mg.).
[7]Lk. 9:23 (J. B. Phillips).
[8]Eph. 5:16.
[9]Gal. 6:1.
[10]*Search the Scriptures* (IVP) and *This Morning with God* (IVP) (in four volumes) question you on the passage for the day, help you to get the most out of your reading and take you through the Bible in three years and five years respectively. Invaluable.
[11]Phil. 4:8 (J. B. Phillips).
[12]2 Cor. 10:5.
[13]Phil. 2:3 (Moffatt).
[14]"In the foreign mission field you must be able to eat a good meal of really unpalatable food whenever needful; enough to keep up your strength for a hard day's work. You can't be fussy there." *Discipleship Which Means Discipline* (Dohnavur Booklet).
[15]Mt. 6:16-18.
[16]Gal. 3:3.
[17]Mt. 2.
[18]2 Pet. 1:6.
[19]1 Cor. 9:25-27 (J. B. Phillips).

Chapter 4
[1]Eph. 3:8.
[2]Mt. 6:33, AV.
[3]1 Pet. 1:11.
[4]1 Cor. 15:57.
[5]Gal. 2:20.

Chapter 5
[1]Mt. 28:18.
[2]2 Cor. 4:7.

[3]Acts 1:8.
[4]Ezek. 36:26-29; also Is. 44:3 and Joel 2:28-32.
[5]Mt. 3:11.
[6]Jn. 7:37-39.
[7]1 Cor. 6:19-20; also Eph. 3:17-19; Rom. 8:9.
[8]2 Cor. 1:20 (J. B. Phillips).
[9]Heb. 10:36.
[10]Heb. 13:5.
[11]Jn. 1:12-13.
[12]1 Jn. 1:8.
[13]2 Cor. 5:14.
[14]Mt. 5:23-24.
[15]Mt. 5:6.
[16]Rom. 6:5; 8:13.
[17]Rom. 7:24.
[18]Rom. 6:6.
[19]Jn. 8:36.
[20]Jn. 7:37-39.
[21]1 Pet. 1:5; Jude 24.
[22]Heb. 10:23.

Epilogue
[1]Rev. 12:11 (Weymouth).
[2]Acts 15:26.

Further reading from InterVarsity Press

TAKE MY LIFE
*Michael Griffiths teaches us to avoid either a "tepid modera-
tion" or a "one-track fanaticism" by observing all Christ has
commanded. paper, $1.75*

NEW LIFE, NEW LIFESTYLE
*Michael Green helps people who have recently entered God's
kingdom and are wondering what the Christian life is all about.
paper, $1.95*

BASIC CHRISTIANITY
*John R. W. Stott presents a clear statement of the fundamental
content of Christianity and urges the reader to consider the
claims of Christ. paper, $1.50*

THE TRIUMPH OF PASTOR SON
*Yong Choon Ahn tells the story of a Korean pastor who was per-
secuted first by the Japanese and then by the Communists; a
story of the triumph of faith under persecution. paper, $1.50*

JOURNEY WITH DAVID BRAINERD
*Richard A. Hasler organizes forty daily meditations from the
diary of David Brainerd and follows each with a prayer which*

encourages commitment to Christ and an active life serving God.
paper, $2.25

KNOWING GOD
J. I. Packer discloses the nature and character of God and how to
get to know him, not only informing the mind but warming the
heart and inspiring devotion. cloth, $5.95; paper, $3.95

UNSPLITTING YOUR CHRISTIAN LIFE
Michael Griffiths applies the last six of the Ten Commandments
to holiness and daily living, suggesting practical attitudes
toward work, recreation and priorities. paper, $1.50

QUIET TIME
Growth in the Christian life originates in daily communion with
God. This guidebook suggests practical methods for a meaning-
ful quiet time. paper, 75¢